Thoughts of Augustus
The Final Poet

To re-order or receive a brochure of
Other available writings
Please write to:

Augustus, The Final Poet
Blessed Love Entertainment
1404 W. Vernon Ave.
Los Angeles, CA 90062
(800) 794-2161

Visit our website for on-line ordering at
www.TheFinalPoet.com

E-mail: AugustusTheFinalPoet@Gmail.com

Thoughts of Augustus

THE FINAL POET

CONTENTS

INTRODUCTION

Currently in Los Angles, California the rate of homicides among African American youth 25 years and under is at 100 to 150 monthly. This is a severe crisis and is in need of immediate attention.

After speaking with several funeral home directors in the city and hearing theses tragic statistics, Augustus, "The Final Poet' decided to reach out to as many of our youth as he could, starting first with his own sons.

Understanding that most of our youth have been conditioned towards material things in life, he had to come up with something that could reach out and snatch their attention. After personal involvement with many of the young men and teenagers in his area Augustus noticed that something was missing. That something was knowledge of their own culture and the true history our African American journey, which has produced in them low self-esteem. In light of this information he tried lecturing regarding the history of African Americans in America but the attention span of most youth is short lived. Therefore he concluded that by combining entertainment with inner-attainment through the medium music and poetry he might have a chance to reach them.

Music and poetry have always been universal arteries that transcend multiple boundaries so he has painstakingly developed his many years of research into poetry and combined it with music. This book is only a mere glimpse into the depths of the thoughts of "The Final Poet."

Our history has been buried far too long and it is high time we dig up and proclaim it to our children that they may live to carry the torch. It would seem that even with the strides and current accomplishments we have made to date within African American communities, the public school systems are still not teaching true African and American history to our children. Sure they have begun to teach regarding slavery but who were we really before there was slavery? Who were we really before we ever knew of America or the English Empire? These works of literature hope to challenge, provoke, and inspire greater depths of personal interest in these areas for anyone who reads them.

Beyond the pages of human history. Can you imagine beyond the pages of history or even one thousand years before written history? Can you imagine the next millennium to come? What was it that has brought us as far as we have come today, what is it that will take us into the tomorrows that will surely come? Many nations held together and remain committed to their unity because they are determined to hold on to their ancestral legacy and continue to build upon it. Should we who are African American's be any less committed because we have been emancipated from the bonds of slavery!

Ex-slaves must return to their original mind. The original mind of the ex-slave is based on the very laws, which govern the universe. When we return to our true source our children will understand that life is the most precious resource they possess.

This book hopes to be that spark which will start a fire in the mind of many for the love of a more positive history for Blacks in the United States of America.

"The Final Poet"

Dedication

This book is dedicated to all the men and women, both young and old who have been instrumental in my development over the years. To my mentors, The Honorable Elijah Muhammad and Minister Louis Farrakhan, who are the constant source of strength and encouragement to me and for me?

To all my children with the hope that the words I have written will serve to enlighten them in their future development and prevent them from ever being deceived or blinded to their true identity as the descendants from those who first walked on this planet.

To my eldest son, Augustus Muhammad, a very special dedication for his constant belief in me and his steadfastness with selling the poetry setting the pace for its national distribution.

To my lovely wife, Phillis, for sustaining me during the composing and compilation of this work, and for her patience and trust during these trying times.

To my secretary Regina Chambers for her diligence with the typing, proofreading, and editing of this book and for understanding the urgency that called for many long hours in order to get the work published.

To all of the descendants of the Ancient Mysteries scattered throughout the world.

Last but not least to my Mother and Father who are deceased in the flesh but alive in my spirit forevermore?

ANCIENT MYSTERIES

Strange divinities walking
The streets of American cities
Strangest of them all
In ghettoes of pity.
They are standing on the earth
Staring into the skies
A people who lost the knowledge of self
In the centuries gone by.
A downtrodden nation
Dwelling in the dust
Now being controlled by
Material things and American lusts.
Pimps, Prostitutes, Hoodlums, and Thugs,

Strung out on sex, over eating,
Alcohol, cigarettes, and drugs.

What happened to these who seem
Lost in religious mythologies?
A spiritual people whose ancestors
Are among the Egyptian deities
Drifting in North America as
One of time's Ancient Mysteries.

The Sphinx and the Egyptian Pyramids
Are small, lasting signs
The peak on the dollar is pointing
To a people separated from
Their place in time
But forever under the scope of
THE ALL-SEEING EYE
In the center of the peak
Focused on the blind nation
Roaming the American streets
Destined to rise to change
The course of history.
Ancient Mysteries

Their great ancestors were
Mothers and fathers of science,
Mathematics, astronomy, and philosophy,
Yet they roam in America as
One of time's Ancient Mysteries.
Laden with agony after crossing
Thousands of highways of good and
Bad civilizations.

The Ancient wise and knowledgeable nation
Constantly moving forward with strong
Determination and devotion to time
And love with attention on
The Universal God they saw above.
Their leaders, preachers, teachers, and
Parents still stand on the earth
After slavery in America as
The strongest people there ever was.

After striving and struggling through
Centuries of humiliation
There are soon to be rewarded and applauded
As the world's strongest nation.
Discrepancies have broke out of other
Nation's minds concerned with the will
Of the ALL-SEEING EYE.
Little consideration for a people's
Separation from their place in time,
Is the extirpation of humanity's humility.
Blind to this nation
As the future masters of human destiny.

ANCIENT MYSTERIES
A nation standing in North America
As the world's oldest family
Denied all knowledge of their own
People in history.
Yet like a chandelier, they are
Hanging from the ceiling of time
Among the ancient mysteries
Of the super mind.

North America! A world
That has existed without the spiritual light.
A mental, moral, and spiritually
Dark house where this nation slept
For over 400 years of fading into
The twilight of oblivion
With no past recollections
Wandering from city to city
Without unity or any serious directions.
Lost in obnoxious psychological darkness
Trapped in the west
Driven like wind without any rest.
No place to flee
For the whole nation
Has lost its memory.

Obliteration! Forgetfulness in the
Land of America where
They failed to remember themselves as
The world's tallest and oldest timber
Forced to worship somebody white
After 310 years of slavery in
The cold month of December.

In the west, the land of trial,
Tribulation, and test,
Just an obstacle course designed
For the best
Being driven by European pests
And made to practice their evils,
Their wickedness, their crookedness,
And everything less.

Not knowing that the time was
Set under Eastern skies by
THE ALL-SEEING EYE
Who told prophets to prophesy of
THE RISE OF THE BEST
FROM OUT OF THE WEST
At the end of 50 thousand years of
REST!!!

50 thousand years is how long
They have been asleep.
The last 5 hundred years was under
The control of human beasts.
Mindless and heartless America
Investigating things beneath the earth
And in the sky.
Things divinely protected by
THE ALL-SEEING EYE.
Yet America is unable to see
That what America has enslaved is
Times most Ancient Mystery

ANCIENT MYSTERIES

OLD, ANCIENT, MYSTICAL, UNKNOWN
ANTIQUES
Walking American Streets
Down on the beat and laying on the beach
All around the America's coast lines
In the summer times
Getting a little sunshine.

NEGROES!
Descendants of the super mind.
NEGROES!
The oldest people in time.
NEGROES!
The sons and daughters of the
ALL-SEEING EYE
NEGROES!
The seeds of the old ancients
Who put the Sun in the sky?
A people whose beginning was so long ago
The truth of their real history
Will bust the minds of
Aristotle, Socrates, and Plato.
The things Negroes built
This modern world will never believe
That is why they are standing
In North America as one of time's
Ancient Mysteries.

Every day the sun rises and shines
In its golden splendor
Glorifying its old ancient Negro masters.
Children of the old Ancient Deities
Walking in the wilderness of
The western hemisphere
Examining the philosophies of
America's colleges and universities
Wondering how could
White pest teach this mess
Called the American modern text.
They would come out better

If they taught the truth

About the knowledge
The Greek Philosophers
Stole from me and you
Knowledge from Jet Black Egyptians
Masters of mathematics, religions, science,
And all of the other intellectual disciplines
And adventures of man.
THE SUMMUM BONUM
THE GREATER AND SUPREME GOOD
THE PURPOSE OF PHILOSOPHY,
IMMORALITY
With ancient deities dwelling in
North America as time's
Ancient mysteries.

BLACK KING

From the cities
Of North America
He is now raising his head
To pursue the mystical path
Leading to the mystics of
His own legendary fame.
A man who knows that
The present course of
Life must be changed.
As time continues to liberate
Him from the bonds of passion
The revelation of his past
Consciousness is not a fashion.

The astrophysical dynamics of the Universe
Is where the mind in him once roamed?
But he has experienced a
Castration of his memory

Which has made it hard for him to see
That he was the Master
Architect of humanity.
(Just a casual point for scientific controversy)

The king is mentally dead
Yet and still the most notable exception
Who built from the darkness?
Of sleeping ignorance
The past's most magnificent community
And surrounded himself
With peace, tranquility, order, and harmony.
He is the origin of time
Presiding in North America
With the indestructible mind
Possessing the highest form
Of electrical energy
His brain is now flowing
With streams of higher subtleties.

Far beyond your
Earthly theories of philosophies
Even though he is sleep
He is still the King.
Beyond all the world's
Thoughts, visions, and dreams
When the first thought moved

Out of the dark
A black man was self-created.
Long before the creation
Of the sun, moon, and stars
He stood in darkness.
He walked upon darkness.
He was the first Black King
And from the fire of his intelligence
He was able to create everything.

He was the beginning of time
who created within himself
The first master mind.
He didn't even have a name
And the human color he chose
Was from the darkness
Out of which he came
Supremely sane.
As he emerged from the dark
Shaking his head to fill space with stars
The first black man is everybody's King
Wise and supreme
Creator, master, and mover of everything.

It will be absolutely mesmerizing
Once the world comes to know
That the descendant of this black God
Is the American so-called-Negro
Who put himself to sleep
About 50 thousand years ago

And 44 thousand years later

Made from himself his greatest foe
Who managed to conquer and abase
The Black King
Down to his lowest low.
The mind in him had to die
And every thought of his greatness
Had to be crucified
And the evidence is every time
You look in the Negro eyes
You can see the King mentally dead
And won't wake up
Even, if you drop a bomb on his head.
Yet it has been divinely prophesied
That at the end of 50 thousand years
The world will experience
The Black King's rise.

O' Mighty Black King
Beyond 50 thousand years ago
There is your history
Stacked back to your beginning
As the head of every dynasty.
A past that consists of so many
Trillions of dreams you made reality.
The universe is your throne
Everything in space around you
Is what you own.
Heaven was inside your head at a
Time when darkness was a physical bed.
Paradise was your actual home
Until inside yourself
You found something wrong

And this is why
You put yourself back to sleep
To pull from within you
Your greatest enemy
From the beginning to eternity
50 thousand years is just a peep
Into the vastness
Of your original mentality.
It is your black beginning
Records cannot find.
50 thousand years
Is just a miscarriage of time
Where ignorance was a pillar
That let you return within to get
The world's most evil and deadliest killer.
The grafted master of deception and lies
Made from within you,
A whole race who hates
Righteousness and truth.
The embodiment of
World envy and hate
Made from within you

To bring about your fate
Only on the earth
The planet you choose
For your foot stool
Not too far
From the planets Venus and Mars.
Your blood relatives
Always full of fun
Everybody travelling together

In orbits around the sun.

Mighty Black King
The past 50 thousand years
Has been one long nightmare
Inside you own universe
Which weighs 11 2/3 quintillion pounds
238 quintillion miles round
Why are you still walking around
In the wilderness of North America
As a slave with your head hung down?
Where is your cosmic robe?
Where is your universal crown?
Something is terribly wrong
You're still gang banging
With saggy pants on.

The King of the universe
Is who and what you are
From the beginning to eternity
You are the master of everything you see.
Your soul is built on truth and reality.
The universe of light
Is only a wheel
You created for yourself to live.
She draws her energy
From the core of your soul.
Ever since you called her out of darkness
And made her roll

From within the

Black walls of space
Spinning for you
Out of your own divine grace
And now she feels sad and alone
Since the original mind in you
Has been gone so long
And now the whole
Universe moans and groans
Praying for you black man
To return to the throne.

Mighty Black King
Your sub-conscious scope
Is incomprehensibly beyond
The scientist of this modern world
Without deception you possess
The highest state of mind;
And this history is alive
And waiting on all the deep thinkers
Who dare voyage through
All the mysteries of time.
Man's vocabulary of words,
Dictionaries, glossaries, and lexicons
Under recorded that under your black feet
The earth weighs 6 sex-trillion tons.
They never knew the age of the sun
They only knew that the mind in you
Was forever working
Like a magic wand.
They saw the pyramids
And the sphinx
Sitting up for thousands of years

In African sands
Demonstrating the power
In your mind as
The original Black Man.

And they have never been able to see
The past, present, or future vastness of
Your original mentality
Because they think
Your mind is still dead and won't wake up
Even if they drop
A bomb on your head.
But this is the day they all shall dread
When God comes on the scene
With good news for the Negro King
Making it known
That this is the time for you
To return to the throne
As the universal master of everything
Black King.

BLACK HISTORY – MY ANCIENT MOTHER

As I cast my eyes
Across the sea of tomorrow
Long are the days,
Long are the nights

I think deep within the silence
Of my soul
Where my mind and spirit

Wades in the sea of my past memory.
I find myself falling in love
With things I already see, within
The magnificent mother of wisdom
Ancient Black History.

As I listen to hear and distinguish
The many sweet and wonderful voices
Echoing across my brain
I long within in my soul
Just to know the names.
The further I look is the further I see
Great Black Kings, Queens, and Kingdoms
Lingering centuries of distance
Behind me.

O' Black History
You are my dear ancient mother
The Queen of my destiny
You've given me dreams to dream.
Your tongue has carried your voice
And your lips have gave it wings.
You've nourished my spirit
With the strength of an Eagle
That flies across the Sun
While my foot tracks are being received
By the earth which weighs
Trillions and trillions of tons.

O' BLACK HISTORY,
You are my vast sea and sleepless mother.
Your love drives me from within

And keeps me always ready to go
With strong determination to learn about
Everything I do not know.

The sails of my eagerness are
Always full and set
Indeed I feel blessed to receive my quest.
My visions are sweeping my mind like the wind
The waves of my discretion
Await the compass of proper direction.
There are so many things I've yet to learn
Just knowing you better
Is my greatest yearn
O' BLACK HISTORY
How often have, I sailed in my dreams
On a ship all by myself
Through the wild winds of stormy weather
Without a compass or telescope
In sadness, pain, and loneliness
But without regret.
The storm of my inner world
Of thunder, lightning, violent winds,
Hail and heavy rain attempt to drive me insane
And this my will, will never let, or prevent me
From learning what I haven't learned yet.

O' BLACK HISTORY
Let the mighty winds blow
I'm determined to learn what I do not know
Although many fragments of my spirit
Have been scattered in the streets of the world
My eyes yearn to see the things I've never seen.

O' black history
You're the Queen of my most, deepest dream
As a son of my ancient mother
Sometimes I cry
As I ride the tides of time in my mind
In hours when my soul feels empty and dark
On the endless journey that I have embarked
But as a man living in a land so strange
I know that I'm just passing through
O' BLACK HISTORY
I'll forever love you.

BLACK QUEEN

Beyond the pages of
Human history
Long before the starlight of the galaxy
You were standing in
Total darkness with me.

Knowledge of the path
Leading to the past of our beginning
Was lost
From our records and our memory.

Our long, long journey
From planet to planet
Should never be taken for granted.
It is the incredibly unexplained
And the most mysterious of all theology
Unable to be reached by man's
Strongest philosophy or terminology.
Because we were as gods
Who left out foot prints
Among the stars
As we proceeded toward the nobility
The marvelous majesty of our
Magnificent destiny
Holding hands to meet the challenge
Of our everlasting, endless eternity
The whole universe is the domain
Of our ceaseless infinity.
And for our crowns
We wore the Milky Way
The well know name for this galaxy
And this solar system for us
Is our present dynasty.
O' Black Queen
You are the woman of wonders
Supernaturally supreme.
You are the highlight of the universe
And the irresistible glory of

Your Black King.
Incredible as it may seem
You're my heaven in manifest reality
And I have always loved you
With the strongest of my memory.
All the way back when
The first thought broke in the dark
Spinning to create the first brain
And heart, a simple atom building itself
Into a spark
Which arched down the dark
With magic and grace
As gods we were able to walk on space
The only history no man can trace
From that hidden and secret place
The womb of darkness that gave birth
To the Lord and Master of the Universe.
We rose in the dark from the earth
A planet composed of water and dirt
So there is no confusion in our minds
About who got here first.

O' Black Queen
The knowledge in you and I
Has never been confused.
"N-E-W-S" does spell news.
North, east, south, and west
Information of directions
That came from me and you.
Knowledge from us
For our unborn generations to use
But long after the study of black self

We learned to reproduce
Way back then when
The first moment in time began
For trillions of years before
GOD created the sun
You and I became
Masters of education

Together we walked on water, land, and sand
You were my woman and I was you man;
But long before we came to walk on ground
We had created for black self a heavenly crown
Composed of every planet and all the stars
Bound in the everlasting togetherness
With the infinite commitment to never part
For all that we see was and is
A creation from our big, red, bleeding hearts.

O' Black Queen
Thank you for ever being
The most beautiful woman I've ever seen.
You've treaded the palace
Of my most, deepest dreams.
Thank you for being with me as we traversed
Between the dark walls of the universe
And God only knows how many times
You and I have walked around the earth
Wearing our heavenly crown
Of planets and stars in the galaxy
Possessing hearing and sight
That had no depths nor boundary
And sheer inner powers of fantastic ability

Even though we fell into hell
To experience the worst of human tragedy
During the dark, weary centuries of
U.S. slavery.
A government in a country
Seeking to make our destiny
A white universal democracy
By forcing us to give up
The knowledge of our black self
And our glorious past identity.
A community of white enemies
Only six minutes old
A cold race who rose to control our soul.

I don't think they know
That our thoughts began to flow
About 84 trillion years ago
6 trillion years before
GOD created the sun,
And 12 trillion years before
He filled space with stars and planets.
They don't know
That the power of our thoughts
Can melt the snow
And sink their world into the Atlantic
Like the Titanic.
We will make the earth shake from
Under their feet
And flood their cities
From mountain peaks.
We'll make their homes and cars
Float down their streets.

We'll raise the clouds from the sea
And make thunder and lightning
Talk to 'em for you and me.
Tornados and hurricanes
Will drive all their multitudes insane
Until they learn to pronounce
Our original names
And realize that the forces of nature
Obeys the Blackman's command.
Even though we are still psychologically asleep
The forces of nature are still obedient
To you and me.
We are the givers of life and death
Therefore they should not make us angry
Or else none of them will be left.
And we, as the gods they shall soon see,
We are the Masters of Universal calamity.
O' Black Queen
We are living in the time of change
And the enemy is using you against me.

He wants your black womb
To give him color biologically
When reproducing him is not
Your responsibility.
I am your Black Man in this land and the King
Of this planet. You are my Black Queen
Who should never take my love for granted
Especially now that I have the key to self-mastery
I'm headed toward the endless destiny
But I won't go anywhere
Without my Black Queen standing there.

The woman of wonders
Supernaturally supreme
Strolls across my soul
In the palace of my most deepest dream
Crowned with the planets and a wilderness of stars
Moving and revolving lights of our galaxy
Cloaked in the Universal Robe of Royalty.
My most Glorious Black Queen
The most beautiful woman I've ever seen
Crowned and bound to be with me
Forever in the everlasting endlessness of eternity.

BLACK QUEEN II

There is much to talk about
In the first atom of life there is no doubt
Everything you ever were, everything you will ever be
Is inside the atomic structure
Composing you and me.
Science and logic bears witness
To your and my atomic vastness.
The black human being is time's true king and queen.
We are the true masters of all things unseen,
Gravity, electricity, sound, and the wind
With mathematics our most precious friend.

We are biologically the possessors
Of every atom in the universe; Atoms
That can only be seen by thought alone.
The unseen powers our ancestors used
To choose the earth for our home
Paradise and heaven as our eternal throne.

Take a look at the atoms.
The fire atoms composing the sun
Created and generated by
Supreme precious wisdom
And man stands in every blaze of every rays
Every day from dust till dawn
Manifesting the will
To rule the entire creation.

But our will is the wheel of thought.
The wheel that has been still for the past
50 thousand years because the mind in us lost the
Will and desire to live
In the North American cotton fields.
And corrupt cities built with stone and steel
And there is only one appeal, which is
A thought you were never taught
About the soul that could not be
Bought and a way to the world

No eye has ever seen reserved
Only for tribe of gods.
A path beyond America
Treaded only by

Black Kings and Queens.
O' Black Queen
Every time I look at you my eyes
Come wide open and my pupils dilate
Helping me to see Heaven standing in front of me.
You are appealing to my eyes far beyond the
Heaven in the sky. A heaven I can't reach or
Get to until after I physically die.
For trillions of years
I have loved you just as you are.
Every time I look at you
My head feels like it's been hit by a star.
You are my universal conclusion and my
Experience of loving you
Has never been some hidden delusion.
And since the other races got here
Your very presence has created in them
A deep confusion and long, sad illusions
Because the men of every race goes
To bed with dreams of a Black Queen in their head
Until morning comes to make them dread that
All night long they got mislead.
You are the heaven that belongs to me.
Black Queen you are the mirror of my destiny.
Time could not favor me more
Even if my future had no door.
You are the door
To that enchanted palace of nature
And in that palace of nature
I see you pure and true
The precious work of art only
Nature could produce

And according to nature itself
You're the only reason
I will never see death.

O' Beautiful Black Queen
Come and go with me
Into the preponderance of the things
Your physical eyes have never seen.
Let me show you the light
Beyond 50 thousand years ago
Where memory of our ancestors
Will thunder inside the walls of our conscious
The knowledge we don't know
And what we learn shall never be forgotten
And their voice an eternal echo
Reminding us of our universal consciousness
In this wilderness where 50 thousand years
For you and I was only one nights rest.
Behold! The Entire Universe
While our feet are planted in the earth
360 degrees of Natural Atomic Mentality
Behold! The reflection of the water
Called the sky, and the mind within you and I
Behold! The brain that contains
12 melanic tracks
7 ½ ounces of brain
Dealing only in truth and natural facts
Producing thought that travels
24 billion miles per second
And all you need is the desire to go with me

And a life time to take one journey
Across this galaxy.
With the power of majestic concentration
And your vast meditation
The earth enjoys a fast and steady rotation.
Started about 76 trillion years ago
Memories locked away
For our historical contemplation

Just like the moon which controls your womb.
According to the long endless line
Of black dynasties locked away
In the memories of these histories.
The moon pulled gods, angels and prophets
From your black belly in every era of time
And as far as we know
With our ego
This started 66 trillion years ago
When the moon was departed from the earth
Until the rule of evil had come to and end
And you gave birth to gods of good
So that a new rule could begin.

O' Black Queen
Come and go with me, don't
Be deceived, don't be fooled by
The evil of my enemy
Because the life that we have *right now*
Is at the cross roads
Between our history and our destiny.
Come and go with me
Take my hand, I am your Black Man.

Incredible as it may seem, I'm about
To fulfill all of your dreams
And show you what it means
To experience paradise and heaven
From now to eternity.
First let me open your eyes
By giving you knowledge of the time.
You see 50 thousand
Years ago I lost my mind
And fell into hell
It was a long mental and spiritual dark night
50 thousand years ago.
I lost my sight and was unable to see
That you were my destiny.

My thoughts frequently fill my eyes with tears
When I think about how I treated you
During the past 50 thousand years.
I had a meeting with death
From who I learned to master my fears
To build my will into an eternal mind
That shall always live.
Incredible as it may seem I rise today
Your everlasting Black King.
When you close your eyes
To look inside yourself
And you humble your mind
To let you thoughts flow free
And your thinking is moving quietly
With the earth from the west to the east
What is it you're trying to see?
Trillions of years of time

Which started with you and me
The universe built on our love
Packed with planets and stars inside every galaxy.

When you close your eyes
To humble your mind
To let your thoughts flow free
What are you trying to see?
How we made land, water, and stone,
Become flesh, blood, and bone
And the earth became our permanent home
Where the sun's blaze gave us our mellow tone?
The sun is the circle of fire
Created from our burning desire
The intelligence in us is
What electrifies the sun
To make it shine
By the power of a greater light
Coming from within our mind.
When you close your eyes to humble your mind
What are you trying to see?

Is it the course we took
Out of triple darkness when and where time began
With you and me trillions of years ago, we made it so,
So why focus upon so much history
Oh my dear Queen, there is no need to look
So far back when darkness and
Space contained the presence
Of you and me before light was
You and I were time's magic seed
And from water and dust we created us

In Beautiful Black Bodies with minds well pleased,
We made the earth turn
With constant pace and proper speed
Creating friction and sweeping winds of time
In which we breathe.
We created our own atmosphere and ears
To hear the sounds of creation and our
Minds possessed with vision
And imagination and have you thought of all the
Times you and I multiplied self into
A nation billions strong!
Is this the reason why when you close your eyes
You have to think so long?
When you close your eyes with the setting of the
Western sun, watching the majesty
Of the world's horizon, when the sky softly
And gently kisses the sea
Do you wonder about destiny
And eternity or the path of life
Where love is leading you to me
And the more your thoughts soar
You can hear my voice from the ocean's floor.
A melody that moves
Smooth as the ocean's roar
And the rhythm of words
Rolling from the waves of my lips
Echoing across your mind

The man you've known since
The beginning of time.
One you shall love always and forever
BECAUSE GOD is DWELLING INSIDE.

When you close your eyes
What are you trying to see?
The ancient memories of our
Magnificent history
Or the life destiny guaranteed
Or how time has bound us together
With love as life's reality.
Bounded by the everlasting togetherness
With love stronger than a mountain
Setting by the sea
Or the eternal memory of how life
And love keeps leading
You back to me
And so time has proved you
To be my greatest reality.
Consider the galaxy
Destiny is calling on you
To dignify our children
And embellish their minds with truth.
America is a material civilization
And sex is her greatest temptation
Mixed with music as motivation
For an entire generation
Turning to drugs to make hard times fly
Smoking poison death
Only to get high
Regardless to how hard we try
Our human spirit is bound to die
Thinking self to satisfy
Unable to share unselfishly
Because we don't see eye to eye.

O' My Dear Black Queen
Consider this galaxy established as our work
Of art and our kind of activity but imagine
Yourself standing with me on the crossroads
Between our dateless past and future destiny.
We cannot live by
The calendar produced by Rome
Since the earth is known to be
The Black Man's home and no race
Knows how long.
They strive to make the Black Man
Wrong with some super information they
Stole before finding the ancient scrolls
And they went to work
Reducing solid Black Kings and Queens
To mixed blood, blank mind Negroes.
And here in North America we are
Still filled with soul and thrills
As Masters of the most
Treacherous and tragic years
And it is our rise God is using
Like a handkerchief
To wipe the tears from the
Nation's eyes because America thinks
She has outgrown God
And has become too big with greed,
Arrogance, and pride, and out of ignorance,
Jealousy, and envy
She wants black and white to stand
Before God side by side
Hoping the whole world will

Continue listening to her lies.
O' Beautiful Black Queen
Consider the life of you and me
Traveling in motion within this galaxy
And consider the time when our
Life was 100% free

Always wearing your crown of
Rubies, diamonds, and gold.
Common to see you every day gliding across palace
Floors in your amazing Royal Robe.
And just to talk about you historically
Is like watching the glory of the
Globe unfold.
Why put up so much
Resistance when the truth about
You is long before any other race
Came into existence. As we are now
On the west end of the earth
And the north corner of the planet your
Subconscious is a god put sound asleep
In a country of 12 thousand
Cities, and dangerous streets.
The Roman calendar say it is the
Year 2015, but according
To the data of my own
Psychological scope, which
Is beyond all the books
I read, life was the beginning
Of light in the darkness
Of one magic seed and

Sometimes it's hard to
Explain the history after
Being born biologically in a
Society controlled by the darkness
Of traditional symbology.
But I believe I have been blessed
To have mental and spiritual eyes
Able to see and comprehend
The beginning of time
When life was the light
Dictating and orchestrating
The very beginning of man.
I am attempting to explain what I can

I appreciate you allowing me to
Share with you what I've seen
My Dear Queen
The reality of my thoughts
And what they have brought
Concerning you and me
Are sometimes only perceived
By what I see in visions and dreams.
Perhaps meditation and concentration
Feeds my imagination
Without abbreviation within
The translation or transliteration
Of one's deepest scientific observations
Produced by the study of self in time.
It's just another joy to share with you
What comes to mind as every generation
Deserves proper education.
Like there is a mind in me which

Carries me back beyond antiquity.
And I'm always trying to understand
The glorious things I see
Like seeing you standing in every path
Of MY inward journeys.
Regardless to how far back
I travel into the past
You were standing there
Queen of my atmosphere
So you mean more to me than my
Own vision and dreams
Even when they come from the stars
Because your existence is the creation
Of the woman of my heart.
I beg you to please listen to me
Especially when the spirit
Moves me through heaven and open space
Into a magnificent, magnifying,
Mysterious, yet majestic and sacred place

Embellished with the rewards from the
Royalty of Our Ancestors who were the gods
Walking with THE GOD in divine grace.
A place where our language changed
And light shone from within our face.
Where the smell was paradise, eternal,
Harmonious, and peace was the taste.
It's the world most beautiful found only within.
It's big enough for two
As long as you are My Queen and
My Eternal and Internal friend
With passionate love coming from within.

We are living in a society that's sinking
You and I should start thinking
About the greatness of our
Children as our higher self
Their conscience will be imbued
Without boundary or depth
And together we shall see the
Benevolent moments of the rare ecstasy.

O' Black Queen
Now is the time to experience and
Explore the fact that every heart
Has a secret door that leads to the
Innermost mysticism of the soul
The closer you get to the core.
The purest and truest light humbles
The intellect that's always seeking more.

YOUNG BLACK BROTHERS
STOP KILLING EACH OTHER

Reality is not as cold as the graves
That consumes your souls
So many **young black brothers**
Have lost their lives
From walking the wrong roads.
Now they will never know
What it means to become a man
Who lives to grow old

And you really don't know
What life is all about
Walking through the days

With your minds and spirits
Buried in hostile and bitter frustrations
Produces by the hurt and agony
From years of black self-doubt
And it is hard for you to change
When the life you live is caught up
And committed to gangs.

If only you would use the power in your brains
Life can become a beautiful thang.
The brain in you is supposed to be
Much greater than THE SUN
Which should remove the thought
That your success in life
Depends on the money you get
From dealing drugs and gun
Young black brothers.

These words are not intended to philosophize,
Conceptualize, or to theorize your life,
But to encourage you to think twice
About the value of another brother's life
Before you roll the dice.
This is the year 2002.
Now how would you feel with a bullet
Coming straight toward you?
This is a whole new millennium
And your future looks bleak
With so many **young black brothers**
ROLLING the streets packing your heat.
Somewhere in the black community
Where you refuse to listen

To the voice of love and black unity.
It is your immaturity and your pride
Increasing the homicide

Leaving thousands of **black mothers**
With tears in their eyes.
Every month in Los Angeles alone
Over **100 Teenage Brothers**
Get sent to their eternal home;
They felt like they had to die
While the gunshots during the night
Made **Little Babies cry.**

You Black Brothers
Please listen to me and allow me
To help ease your pain.
Take yourself a long walk, in sunshine or rain
Because after you finish reading this poem
And the words it contains
Designed for the Nature of your brain
You may never think same.

The older black brothers
Got caught up in the government's thang.
Since the end of the Viet Nam WAR
They came back looking like
Their minds were trapped in a JAR.
Confused with a **VIOLENT ATTITUDE**
UNEDUCATED BLACK SOLDIERS
SELLING TONS OF HEROIN AND COCAINE
It WAS the white man's game
For our older brothers to come back
Living without hope, using and selling dope

TO their own black folks.
Now AMERICA is about to choke
Because freedom for NIGGAS
Is just a word stuck in her throat
And the lack of money for you has become
Like a rope around the neck of the black community,
WHO STILL REFUSE TO LISTEN TO THE
VOICE OF LOVE AND BLACK UNITY.

Our **older black brothers**
Trained to destroy, trained to kill
And now their greatest fear
Is making the right change,
Which is to stand up for you and me
And teach us universal truth.

But as you take this long walk on city streets
Think about the earth rolling under your feet.
Rolling toward the sun
You see rising from the east.
Think about the brain in you
Being actually greater that the sun
And how one thought from your brain
Is greater than the atomic bomb.
And you might want to ask
This government about
Its reasons for manufacturing guns.

Young black brothers
Here in California
You are as far west as you can get
Speaking the English language

Without learning the original
Language of the ancient black alphabet
And you haven't learned enough yet
Life walking in the rain
Without getting wet.

Real knowledge is what you need
Circulating inside your brain
So when you see the wind
You can make it change.
Talk to the weatherman and place your bets.
Then create the greatest storm telescopes
And radar ever met.

Young black brothers
Stop killing one another
What do you need with guns?
When the brain in you is greater than the sun
Which constantly moves the earth
Which weighs trillions of tons
Traveling over a thousand
Miles per hour using her water
To make it rain
For the God inside yourself
possess power to make it shower
The mind in you should stand
Above the tallest tower
Unlike the older brothers
Who were reduced beneath the flowers
So they never obtained the knowledge
Beyond public college.
They worked all week long

Only to enjoy nightclubs, discos
And Sunday religious folly.

They couldn't be about the
Black original God living within
And still be employed by their
So-called white friends
Who laughed at them work
With no knowledge of the earth.
A people older than the sun
And older than the entire universe.
They had empty minds and empty souls
Broke away from the ancient knowledge
And ancient stories they were never told.

Like the times of the Black Empires
And millions of **Black Dynasties.**
When the earth was paradise
With the fresh clean air to breathe

Able to live to be a thousand years old
Masters of the heat, controllers of the cold,
The builders of planets,
Now called Niggers and Negroes.
Tricked to leave his throne
500 years ago, history has shown.
And now it's time
For You **Young black brothers**
To put your robe and crown back on.
But the first thing you must see
Is that America did you wrong!
Only allowing you to make big money

With sports, rap, and singing songs.
But as you read this poem
You know it won't be long
Before you are on your way
Back to the throne where you belong.
The earth is your original home.

You will have freedom to navigate
Real space once again.
Returning happiness to your relatives
On other planets hearing them
Ask you, "Where have you been?"
And you will tell them
I fell into hell and my mind
Went to sleep for 49 thousand years
Among African beast?? And 500 years
Roaming American streets.

So when you stand up on your feet
From California, LOOK AT the EAST AS
The truth unfolds
About your universal crown
And you universal robe
Your right possessions white folks stole

Of course you have to become bold
TO DEAL WISELY
WITH THE WICKED SCIENTIST
Seeking to steal your soul.

**Young Black Brothers
Stop Killing One Another**

Take yourself a long walk, in sunshine or rain.
You've got to think hard
To forgive and overcome your pain
The earth is still rolling under your feet
Learn to show natural love
Without playing games or packing heat
And above all understand one thing,
If you're black in this universe
Your ancestors are all the same.

So go and look at yourself
In your mirror and strive hard
To overcome your pain and make the change.

Young Black Brothers
Stop Killing One Another
Rolling the streets, packing your heat,
Calling yourself and dog
And calling your woman
An itch with a capital "B"
Possessing the only brain of infinity
Born to become masters of
Universal destiny.

But your mind is buried deep
In personal and public confusion and lies
About your proper identity.
The hate inside yourself.
Is easy for you to see
Which is what's at the root
Of your own envy and jealousy.
But you blame your brothers

For your own insanity
Which is at the root of the reason
Why killing your brother
Is done so easily.

When overcoming the pain
Of your own frustration and bitter hostility
Strive to educate another brother

Opposed to sending another brother
To the penitentiary or the cemetery.

This is a new millennium
And each brother's destiny is to be free!!!

But you need vision and imagination
In order for each brother to see.

That now is the time for him to master
And control his own destiny
By first understanding that history
Is the foundation of today's reality.

CRUSH "THE BLACKMAN"

It's built in the fibers of American life
Centuries of pain and endless sacrifice.
Unable to lift his head with any measure of pride
Working for free with only time and God on his side.
Being brought westward to America's land
Where a whole world was built
On crushing "The Blackman."
Since 1555 the Blackman has cried
And no nation, no where
Ever saw the tears fall from his eyes
No nation, no where
Ever knew the hurt of his troubled soul

The fall from being an Ancient Black King
To being the American slaves
Called Niggers and Negroes.

The story of his greatness has never been told
And the memory of when he was in power
Was erased from the face of the globe.
And America wanted no one to know
Because Euro-Americans thoroughly understand
That this country became No. 1 superpower
From crushing "The Blackman."

America's theology is trick-know logy
The study of a mystery God
Somewhere beyond the sky
A philosophy like a heavy dark blanket
Just thrown over her black slaves mental eye
Deceived to believe that in all of her wars
BLACK should be first to die
And after 460 years, millions of Negroes
Still believe in this bald-face lie.

Even though we all know about
The U.S. slave trade from 1555 to 1808
Black people are still trapped in America
Without a freedom date.
Americans do not care!
Black men working in the pen,
Black women working on low paying jobs,
Food stamps and welfare,
All of this was a master plan
To build this white western world
On crushing "The Blackman"
So when we hear the cry of voices from bones
Covering the bed of the Atlantic Ocean
It's not long before our emotion

Sets us in motion with GOD'S divine notion
From the African shores to the American sand
Where all of us will take our final stand
With one divine demand which is
A full and complete freedom
For every Blackman

WHAT I HEAR and WHAT I SEE

I hear the voices of civilization
Spoken by the lips of history.
Wouldn't you be surprised to know
What I hear and what I see?
The typical and secondary senses
Of universal authority.
The strange and curious legends
That prepared us to face coming difficulties.
The enemy who says black history is a thing
In which there is no real value to see.
A world full of evil people
Who made slaves of you and me?
The mightiest black nation
Chopped down like a tall oak tree
The greatest black people of Africa
Destined to roam the wilderness of streets,
Bound to plantations and treated worse than beasts?
Trapped in horrors of hell in every century
Wandering in the western world

With no memory of how mighty they used to be
Lost to the knowledge of self
And everybody else.

I hear screams and loud screams
Coming from the far motherland.
I hear screams and loud cries
Of those victimized
By the greatest evil known to man
I hear screams and loud cries
Of those whose blood soaks the shores
Of Africa and America's sands
I hear screams and loud cries
Of those who became the major plan
Of the Devil disguised as a man

I see the ships coming in
All of my people in chains
Forced to live by another people's culture
Forced to wear another people's names.
I see a slave running
The slave is trying to get away.
I see the slaves on plantations
Working hard every single day.
I see the slaves on the plantations
During the night, the slaves are trying
To pray, I see slaves suffering
Through the centuries working
Like animals without pay.

I see slaves of 2016
Still waiting for
That better and brighter day.

The mind in you has been reduced
And you have been made to hate the Truth.

It has become hard for you to comprehend
Yourself as being once among the gods
Possessing the mind power
To walk upon the dark
But the Truth says that you are the only man
With footprints among the stars.
Even before there was light
Deep and steep in the darkness
Where you were in possession
Of the power to create
Whole galaxies of planets and stars.
And if you start thinking on this
From where you are
To reach your beginning
Might be a little too far
But just think over
The past 50 thousand years
About how you got here.

You fell away from civilization
When you broke away from
Your historical and universal education.
You lost the power
To rule your own creation
When you psychoanalyze your black self.
Your divine ego and conscious personality
Was almost put to total death.
But the ruling nature in you is only asleep
From being emerged deep into the
Preponderance of Hollywood Fiction
Instead of your own historical Reality.
Although you are physically alive

With the Earth rolling under your feet
The knowledge of your Atomic Composition
Cannot be found within your present memory.
Even though you can see the Sun
You can see the planets, the Moon, and Stars
The ruling nature in you is buried
In ignorance behind Steel Methodical bars.
And the only man who has
The Key to Set Free your universal personality
Is known as Allah, The Almighty God.
Go and ask Jesus or Christ
Who never spoke one word of English
And you will see that Hollywood's Fiction
Is Just about Finished.
As you rise from your mental crucifixion
Black shall be forever
A permanent universal tradition
Waiting in every school of education
And taught wisely to the millions
Of unborn black generations.
What a Terrible shame
You have become big with pride.
Lost from the work of fame

Under your slave master's names
And murder of your brother
Is an everyday game.
Filling up city cemeteries
Without feeling any pain.
You're lost in this wilderness
Sick, wild, and insane.
You don't know who to Trust

And you don't know who to blame
And it's hard to tell who is telling
You the honest to God's Truth
When the murderer of your Family
Looks blacker than you
Which is the manifesting fact
Of how far down we have all been reduced.
The present Rise of your Ruling Nature
Is not Hollywood's Fiction
On some Movie Screen.
This has been predicted and prophesied
The rise to your glory is no damn dream!
Biologically it is in your genes.
The very nature of your DNA says
That you were self-created
Then born to be the Universal King.

O' Black King
50 thousand years has been one long night
But there is 84 trillion years dictating our Fight.
And as we collect our strongest thoughts
Without the deception of world emotion
Announce to Every Nation
That King Negro is back in motion
With one foot on the land
And one foot on the ocean.
Standing in the bible as the Son of Man.
Standing in the midst of seven Continents.

The Negro King Rises on Earth in
The midst of the Seven Continents
Stretching forth our hand to the heavens

Saying, time that you know it
The Mystery of God is finished
Because Black was, Black is
And Black shall always be.
Black is Everlasting because Black is Forever.

You have been conquered
And reduced all the way down
To your lowest low
Roaming around in THE wilderness of North America
Thinking of yourself a U.S. Slave
Nigga or a Negro.
And your condition won't change
Until you change what you think you know
Which is worldly knowledge from the pale race
Who has been and still is your greatest foe.

They were clever enough
To turn you from peace to violence
Against yourself
While your heart is bursting
With love for them and everybody else.
Now homicide is on the rise
Of black against black
And you're killing each other
Over a little money and a white
Sack of crack and you never
Thought to think of the root reason
You're acting like that.
Watch the change of the seasons
Life is not a dream.
Listen to the words of the poet

Who talks about you when you were
The King.

NEGRO CHRISTIANS

WHERE ARE THEY FOUND?
They grew up within
American cities and towns.

WHERE ARE THEY FROM?
The became known as
Negroes after slavery
In America begun.

HOW DID THEY BECOME CHRISTIANS?

When the slave master said
Jesus and God were white
The Negro was forced to listen.

WHEN DID ALL OF THIS TAKE PLACE?
After the memory of their past
Had been erased and
All the thoughts of their greatness
Could not be traced and
They had been made to think
That they were African savages,
Descendants of a Sub-human race.

NEGRO CHRISTIANS!

Because they were forced to listen
To worldwide snakes crawling in the garden
Of the globe deceiving the dark nations
By whispering into their original black souls.
Forced to listen to Two-footed snakes
Whose bodies were pale
Who used the name of GOD's PROPHETS
To lead Negroes straight to hell.

When the Europeans came to America
Out of Divine grace
The Red Indians called them
FORKED-tongue and PALE-FACE.
Columbus and his crew
Discovered America in 1492
English speaking people who always
Mixed lies up with the truth.
While Sir John Hawkins
Was headed to Egypt to get me and you

Bringing us to these American shores in 1555

And spent 64 years destroying
OUR ORIGINAL MINDS.

Once their slave making experiment was complete
They went back and forth
Between American and Africa
To get the number of slaves they needed
From 1555 to 1808.
The mad rush to build America
Was something that could not wait.
Come 1865 the eyes of our minds
Were totally blind.
After we worked 310 long years
Without receiving one dime,
They gave us their religion
And forced us to listen.
And since that time we've been known as
NEGROE CHRISTIANS

We are the people
Who came with the Earth
But in America We're treated worse than dirt!
Oh, yes it hurts to be treated evil
When you come to know
Who was on the earth first.
The rulers of churches and public schools
Established these intuitions
To limit our minds
And to make ex-slaves easy to handle
In a future mental grave.
As the centuries rolled by
They put Negro Christian's minds

In the sky.
They kept us blind to the history
Of the ancient world
And our royal road of life
While selling our bodies
For an extremely cheap price.

MENTAL SLAVERY,
MENTAL INCARCERATION,
MENTAL BONDAGE,
MENTAL SERVITUDE.
MIND CONTROL, chains of
MENTAL CAPTIVITY!!!
From 1863 to 2016
This caused us to be ex African Kings and Queens

NEGRO CHRISTIANS

Institutions and organizations
Of Negro Christians
Are the strongest of mind control
Places where the secret mysteries
Of us are never told
The wisdom of Ancient Black Masters
Only seen in signs and symbols.
Our fore parents saw the
Sun, Moon, and Stars,
They saw the clouds floating on high
And rain fall to the ground.
The great lessons
They learned in nature
Kept their minds

From being completely sound
When the rise of the sun taught them
The possibility of thinking freely
The melody of different birds
Taught them how to sing.
Their voices rode across plantations
On the winds mighty wings.
The beauty of their souls

Always puzzling yet more pure than gold
The meditation of their minds
Were astoundingly revealing.
Like the chain of mountains covered in snow
Refreshed their souls with a divine glow.
They had eyes and ears to see and hear.

Deprived of the freedom to know
They lived in pain waiting for
CHRIST TO APPEAR

NEGRO CHRISTIANS.

The product of English Slave Masters
Who knew that Negroes could build America
Up must faster so they opened up a
Negro church and college
Faking like they were
Giving Negro knowledge.
Pretending as though they were
Giving us some real information
After mixing corruption with
Normal EDUCATION

And stirring the Negro's mind away
From himself as a part of the
DESTRUCTION OF BLACK CIVILIZATION.

THE NEGRO CHRISTIANS
Are
ORIGINAL BLACK PEOPLE
Who represent the white world
Because they think the white world
Is the best world for them to represent
With NO QUESTION Of WHERE the
ORIGINAL BLACK WORLD WENT!

LIBERATON OF OUR MINDS

In your mind
When you use your imagination
You can see the earth
As she moves around the sun
A huge planet revolving through space
Carrying over seven billion people
Weighing six sextillion tons
And the orbit in which we travel
Leads us into divine perfection
We are spinning and turning

Into the light after every night
And man has been blessed
With hearing and sight
To see and hear the sounds
Of this, his vast creation.
Possessed with dreams and visions
And frequently gifted with revelations
So that he may know his human destination.
Man has grown to believe
That power is in the barrel of a gun.
Yet man is the trait that transcends time
And the greatest expression of life
Has been and still is the brilliance of his minds,
But today he stands behind
The dark walls of one global color line.

The 20th century
Is the arc and the mark here in human history
Where the mind in us is finally being set free.
A whole hundred years just a period of time
Where the mind in black people
Say no color line.
And as we transcend the old legacy
Of U.S. white supremacy
The way we think is God's own tool
Now being used to uplift
The whole humanity.
Never again to be enslaved,
Terrorized, tyrannized, or monopolized.
This century represents
The liberation of our minds.
In your mind

You can see the moon.
The great balance for our planet
Exactly 48 thousand miles away
Revolving around 28 days

To keep the water of oceans in place.
Like magic the moon and the earth
Moving in the same orbits through space
For the past 66 trillion years.
Just to give you an idea
Of how long black people have been here
Dealing constantly with the dim unknown
Conquering skepticism, superstitions, and fears
During this 20th Century
We put an end to nationwide segregation
And brought forth a new millennial change
That pulled and stretched the limits of
Our moral imagination.
We laid down a new foundation
We created in black self a new determination
We fought and struggled for black people
To obtain proper education.
Unlike the 19th Century,
When law in North America
Said it was a crime
For black to people to read.
At a time when the knowledge of black self
Became our greatest need
Under cruel authorities cloaked in black robes
Of white justice and U.S. democracy.
They never intended for us to see
That they committed the worse crime

In human history, in the name of God
They told us nothing but lies
Concerning our proper identity
And today they are still struggling to prevent
The spiritual opening of our eyes
With lies and more lies.
Work hard Niggers and you shall succeed
In the name of our white Jesus
Get down on your knees
And when you see a whit police

Learn to say please.

But Today
This is not the language to use
With you and me!!!
As this earth continues
To travel around the sun
We have no need to fear or depend on the
White Man's gun.
God is giving us one lesson
And that is that
The thought in us is light, sight, and divine.
The only power we need is
The liberation of our minds.

The days of trouble are here
People everywhere are living in fear.
The land is full of bloody crimes
Violence is on every nation's mind
Except the Negro who now cry
No Color Line.

The earth is the timetable of human history.
The Negro is afraid to take control of his own destiny.
Drugs and guns make Negroes feel
Courageous and bold
Blind to the color line that made him
A stranger to his very soul.
Wise men of great knowledge
Thousands of years ago,
Now confined to a limited mind
In slums, projects and ghettos.
Behold the mind of the Negro.
It's like a deep, dark, black hole
Possessing ungodly spirits; mean,
Ugly, bitter and cold
Waiting for God to remove his woes.

The mind in the Negro
Is a map containing many roads
That led to treasures
Of every man's soul.

Somewhere in our vision and dreams
There are revelations of things unseen.
We may never know what they truly mean
Or what they are trying to say.
As we're passing through troubles of another day
Our hearts forever seeking a new and better way.

We all stand in need of change.
Change the course of our history
Change the life of millions who live in misery.
Change reality from the path of a destructive destiny.

Change the traditional way we believe.
God knows exactly what I need.
Man was created to live eternally.
The change for a better world
Is man's responsibility.
But man is so full of rude insults and hostility
Blind by the evil practice of religious hypocrisy.
Trapped in generations of false pride and vanity,
Engaged in desperate compilation of luxury and
Money; and now, the mind of man is
Stuck in the misery of his own unstable memory.
Lost in his perception of the world's economy.

The mind of man has grown engulfed with lies.
Like acid rain, lies brings pain.
Lies are now driving millions insane.
Lies creep and crawl into your mind
Seeking to destroy any truth it finds.
Lies are expressed with deep sincerity.
Lies have cause whole nations to fall
Like Russia, Japan, and the Berlin Wall.

Lies and disappointments
Cause tears and fears
At the extreme end of good and bad emotions.
Tears and fears produced by intense gladness
Or intense sadness or by heavy confusion and
Outright madness.
One's inner guilt self can't forgive
Always brings fear and tears
Or the harsh rejection of one you've loved
For many years or being delivered

From the mercilessness of one's own fears.

Like a mother watching her son go to
War on the battlefield
And the joy she experiences when he
Returns without getting killed.
The thought of this experience
Could fill your own eyes with tears.
And so we think and wonder about
The cities of North America
Being like Los Angeles
Where we continuously live in danger
Of so many fears waiting for
The liberation of our minds.

CRACK BLINDS YOU TO THE FACTS

Let me on that stage
Cause I'm enraged
I'm another rapper
That's got to get paid.
The mind of the young people
Of this generation got to be saved
From a drug that drags
Young people to early graves.
I'm talking about CRACK!!!
A powerful drug that sets
Your brain ablaze
Every time you hit a pipe
It makes your body wave.

CRACK!!!
You're walking the streets
With a broken mind
Hallucinating on the past, the present, the future.
The past, the present, the future.
See what I mean
You've lost the knowledge
Of your place in time.
All because of CRACK!!!
A powerful drug that sets
Your brain ablaze
Every time you hit that pipe
It makes your body wave.

CRACK!!!
Your real situation is

Stress and strain
So you grab a pipe
To escape your pain.
You smoke on CRACK!!!
Until you forget your own name.

CRACK BLINDS YOU TO THE FACTS

Every time I see you
You're trying to get high
Running from everyday problems
With no wings to fly.
Chemical death moving in your veins
Killing blood cells of
Your young human brain
While confusion drives
You deeper insane.

CRACK!!!
Oppression and depression
Gave your parents the blues.
A hurt generation that
Stayed drunk on booze.
Now war on gangs all over the news,
Children dropping out of school
Thinking nothing to lose.
Like a race of fools
Politicians blaming dope dealers
For the coldest vice ever used.
A powerful drug that sets
Your brain ablaze.
Every time you hit the pipe

It makes your body wave.
CRACK!!!

SUPPOSE

Suppose!!
You can keep your sanity
When everybody around you
Is losing theirs
And blaming the loss of
Their sanity on you.

Suppose!!
You have faith in yourself
At a time when no one
Have faith or confidence in you
But you make excuses for
The lack of Faith and confidence
Others may have in you.

Suppose!!
You are being patience
And don't grow weary waiting.

Suppose!!
You're being hated
For not dealing in lies
Or being hated for not giving in to hate
And you still don't look too good
Or speak too wise

Suppose!!
You can dream
Without making dreams your ruler.

Suppose!!
You can think
Without thinking being objective.

Suppose!!
You can meet with victory and
Destruction, and your attitude toward
Both of these never changes.

Suppose!!
You can handle your most
Honest words being perverted
By reprobate minds who trick
And deceive people who are unwise.

Suppose!!
What you sacrifice your life for
Is destroyed, you have to rebuild it
Without any of the proper tools.

Suppose!!
You can combine your whole life
Accomplishments into one pile
And gamble double to nothing and lose
And start again at your beginning
And never say a word about your loss.

Suppose!!
You can move your
Heart and nerve with fortitude
And strength to work, long after
The spirit in you is gone
And withstand when there is

Nothing in you except
The will which says withstand.

Suppose!!
You can speak to multitudes
And maintain your virtue
Or sit and travel with kings
Without losing your common touch.

Suppose!!
Every man is important to you,
But no man is too important.

Suppose!!
Armies of enemies
Or affectionate friends
Can't harm you.

Suppose!!
You can occupy,
The un-forbearing hour with sixty minutes
Of certainty and fun.

**The whole planet is yours to express
Your manhood, as you complete each journey
Around the sun, my sons.**

IT'S TIME TO TAKE A STAND

When I look into the future
I see the earth full of people
Whose minds and hearts are clean
I see righteous generations that dreams
Of marvelous human impeccable destiny.
But in order to make my visions and dreams become
Tomorrow's reality I must first realize
That I am a man of today
And that It's my time to take my stand.

When my mind possesses
Knowledge and understanding
Of all the mighty and wonderful generations
That existed long before my time

I am thankful for all of the lessons
Which I have learned
From the strong generation that now stands
Just one or two steps behind.
Lessons that nobly equipped my mind
And helped me to recognize the importance
Of being a righteous man.
Lessons that help me to recognize that
It's my time to take my stand.

When confusion has gripped the mind
Of the wisest people who rule this land
The spirit of evil has a strong and mighty hand
And genocide for a nation of people
Has become a number one plan.
The most powerful government on earth
Is now living in a house built on sand.
I am worried as the people of the earth so
Approach the very edge of the most
Dangerous situation ever known to man
Indeed I believe that it is my time to stand.
When the voices of good human leadership
Are still vibrating in the atmosphere
Of the whole entire world
The stage of their perfection lies
Within their resting souls.
It fills my eyes with tears to think of
The sincere inkling of their love
And the wonderful stories their graves never told.
My self-accusing spirit never
Fails to arouse the pangs of my conscience
Every time I make the slightest

Departure from the path of rectitude

I hear ancient and recent voices of men and women
Who died in the struggle of freedom for our people.
Voices that so often echo in the atmosphere
Of my mind here on earth during my own time
Telling me to STOP
Allowing my low desires and animal
Passions to rule my mind.

When my heart each day reflects itself
In the actions of my daily image
I believe that almighty God
Has looked upon me standing in this world
As a man of ordinary intelligence and
Placed in my mind good news
And in my visions I see and hear Good News.
Loud reverberation echoes are heard
Coming from the chain
Of mountains that are within my soul.
I hear the voices of the ancient civilizations
Coming from valleys of old and I see
Storm clouds of human problems
Hanging over the globe
A world of modern society being lost in the
Shadow of the dark cloud that has arose
From ancient time and grown over the skies
Of my conscious mind.
Frequently I have felt less than a man
But all of what I hear and see are only
Signals telling me that
It's my time to take my stand.

For 35 year I had traveled on the wrong road
Looking for God and manhood
Outside of myself
Never realizing that my conscience is the
Sun of my inner world

Which means that my personal savior
Is my own conscience.
Ignorance and confusion has been the dark clouds
In the sky of my mind blocking my inner
Being from the light of understanding
Real knowledge as the only deliverer of my
Inner being.
For 35 years I've lived in a mental and spiritual
Prison and for the first time in my life
On earth knowledge and wisdom
Has come to me from GOD
To guide me from the dark prison wall
Of my own ignorance.
Now I know the value of myself being
An upright man glad to know that
It is my time to take my stand

I am exhorting my individual conscience
To the duty that I owe only to GOD.
Seeking to carry and uplifting message of peace
To my family, relatives, friends, and
The rest of the world.
This is the merit of my own
Internal and external love
Even though some may think that love

And concern are the things that
A black convict should not have.
Since emphasis seems to be placed
Upon where I am
And the way I have lived in the past
I present variations in degrees of
Both emotions of life, love, hate, satisfaction,
And dissatisfaction.
I find that love, peace, and righteousness
In a civilization of both good and evil
Are positive emotions and practices
That run the entire gamut of MY life

From the most primitive to the most unique,
Remarkable and advanced ones.

Often in stress under strange,
Unusual pressure, and circumstances
I call upon the Mind
And Spirit of the God of my
Ancient black ancestors, which did dwell
Devoutly in great kingdoms of peace
Right here on earth.
I find myself seeking nourishment and strength
From the roots of my own past
Deep unlimited history.
Nourishment and strength of wisdom
And knowledge which help me deal
With the controversies, complexes, envious,
Ignorant opinions of people
Who now live here in my own time.
I often call upon my ancestors from

The silence of a deep profound meditation
Asking for their powerful spirit of love
And peace to enlighten, encourage and uplift me
From the darkness of an evil

Environment here at the crossroads
Of history and destiny.
Despite the fact that they and I exist at
Different times and at different places
It is remarkable to observe the same
Essential characteristics of Divine love
Within my ancestors now seemingly to prevail
In my own life
Therefore the turning of my life
With ingenuity is not just the mere
Utterance of words
But it is actually a reality

Here in this time of divine amendment of a
Divine universal change
Which starts for me from within me
It is interesting to observe the service done to limit
The authority of God's divine will.
The service of destroying the element of life
That will insure us all a more satisfactory
Existence as human beings,
The service done to uproot the universal truth.
It is this unrighteous service that has
Produced within me the power
To govern my life with important functions
That benefit us all.

Of course at this time it is obviously impossible
To touch on all the services now woven
Throughout these North American fibers of life
And the life of the whole world.
It is obviously impossible for one to make
An unlimited number of generalizations
Concerning the way we live
In our human environment of life
So large as our National, International
And Universal consciousness.
But the bulk of my thoughts and emotions
During my hard search
To make contact with the spiritual world
Has created a spirit within me
That has moved me into the
Belief and confidence that I can work wonders.
I can build a kingdom
Of real peace and righteousness
Surrounded with pyramids
More modern, more lasting
Than the pyramids of Ancient Egypt.
However, I find myself restricted
By physical confinement and centuries

And millenniums of lies that
Have wrapped my mind up like
And Egyptian mummy.
In spite of all the surmounted obstacles
Of my own history,
My own customs, and traditions,
I am still being moved by the
Great spirits of my great ancestors

Both ancient and recent.
This spirit moves me voluntarily or by force
In the most serious of manners
It has become my motivation among men
Who are lost just as I have been lost

Black men in North America
Are still lost.
Lost behind the border lines of time
That dictates the very beginning of
Psychological slavery.
Lost behind the dark walls of mental danger.
Lost within the confines of their
Own personal history
Unable to cope with life today
Without being followers of those
Who have conquered the greatest men
And nation on the planet earth.
Lost within the confines of the evil
That lingers within their own souls
Lost within the confines of a mind unable
To see that true freedom starts
From within their own selves
Not realizing that the freedom of our
Black ancestors is not just
A historical document
But their past practice of true freedom
Is a powerful and mighty light
That shines upon the conditions of our
Minds enslaved in these modern times.
Frequently I find the Great Spirit driving
Me through a variety of different

Successive stages of my inner development.
I've been presented with a
Favorable set of circumstances.
Circumstances which have allowed the liberation
Of my own mind to become a reality.
Circumstances that have created in me strong

Resentment for treachery,
Lies, deception and false promises.

When the light of history shines upon me
I see myself as the remains of
A mighty black nation
That has been conquered.

Yet the Divine Spirit of peace, love
And righteousness is at work from the
Very core of my very own being
And I know that it's time to take my stand.

As I strive to exercise the art of deep thinking
Along with the skill of emotional management.
The discipline of ordering my
Affairs with excellent consideration,
Deliberation, and ability to manage
My own course of action,
With behavior and conduct according to
My own free will with
The compact concern by which I
Become responsible for the safety of myself
My family, and all those connected
To me in the righteousness of time, and

The True Living God
I find those who love lies and evil are practicing
Hatred and striving to nullify my attempt to bring
Peace to this troubled world
Of human violence and bloodshed.

I heard a great man say that man
Has been in existence for 84 trillion years
I wonder if I can reach that far with my thinking
Behind me is a deep and powerful study
Of man trillions of years, billions of generations
Before me and behind me
Right here on both sides of my own human existence,
I now must take total advantage of my mind's
Liberation and study all of the unseen
Generations both before and behind me.

As time and creation moves on
Surrounding me with billions of great generations
I feed my mind on that whish is above
And below, that which is
Past and that which is present.
I question the prophets of the Holy Scriptures.
I question the scientist and historians
For these I find to be the best students
Of time and creation.
I find the knowledge and wisdom of God
Swelling within me
All the way to the last day of my own
Mental and physical existence.

It is my desire to use the magnificent,

The wonderful, the beautiful,
And remarkable guiding rules of life
During my onward course
Toward the goal of my life.
This is to know the complete truth,
And deal properly with the
Two co-eternal principles of
Darkness and light,
Knowledge and ignorance.
This is to obtain true insight into
The spiritual world of the eternal self
The Great Maker of the heavens and the earth.

As a man moving within this moving creation
I hope to inherit good from the
Divine Supreme Being.
Such as means and methods
To increase the light that I found in the
Darkness of my own being.
Such as my dreams and visions
Of revealed truth that
Continue daily to transform my liberated mind.
Such as spiritual dominance
Combined with my internal political supremacy.
As the veil of evil and hatred is being
Removed from over my heart and eyes,
After my death of ignorance,
I see many blessings already in my life.
Through knowledge of Divine Love
I shake the dust off from my resurrected mind.
Dust is the first stage of my spiritual life.
I find no more need for my mental grave

In the dust of my own ignorance.
Therefore I can now honestly say
That my life of wrong doing is
Undoubtedly a thing of the past.
This simply means that among men of
mental and spiritual darkness
I have been touched by The Light
That only man can serve as a model for men.

Now I have faith in the
LORD OF ALL THE WORLDS
Now it's my time to take my stand.
Even though I cannot show
The things that are coming
I will indeed achieve the end which
I have in view.
I am depending on my own
Growing conscious and discretionary
Powers to govern my biological behavior

Habits that are bad
Within my soul and my spirit
Through intelligence and the light
Of my growing knowledge.
As a man within this moving creation
Beginning to experience the power of the mind
And the production of thought
Ideas have become for me more
Naturally especially when my telescopic hind sight
Is focused upon the work of my ancestors.
How marvelous! How remarkable!
How wonderful were those beautiful

Kingdoms of clean civilizations
Built by the hands of my own great black ancestors.
How interesting it is for me to be
Labeled as one who thinks
With hatred for the white race.
It is interesting to see and experience
The hot frustrations and hatred,
Bitter emotions of evil spirits
Dwelling in men who rise up against me
Like the flamatory flames of the devil's furnace
Simply because I classify myself
A student of time, history, and human destiny.

There were many masters of evil
On earth in the past
And their spirits are prevailing
In these modern times.
Devoutly possessing many men's minds
They become noticeable when
They verbally and physically
Attack the one who represents the
Truth and the life of righteousness.
However as I cast my eyes and thoughts
Back in time I find

The prophets in the immediate past
Millenniums and examine their
Marvelous and wonderful struggle against evil.
I admire their efforts to bring peace to the
Human troubles of their own time.
I see their past struggle as a sign for mine.
The evil in man has grown more and

Become more sophisticated than ever before.
It would take a book over a thousand
Pages to describe the vast differences
Between right and wrong.
In submission to the concept that
The Holy One of Universal Power is needed
To make a clear, total, and thorough,
Complete, and plain difference between
The two human principles, we know
Even he will be called a liar.

Now that my mind and spirit is alive
Indeed I have eyes to see the matter through
Which true love and knowledge is obtained.
I now declare before the world that
The mighty course of evil must change.
There shall be no fellowship
Between righteousness and unrighteousness.
There shall be no communion
Between Light and darkness.
There shall be no brotherhood between
Knowledge and ignorance,
Wisdom, and foolishness, nor Life and death.
As a whole we must find the
First step and take that first step
And realize that
It is now time to stand.

That first step is truthful and honest
Social relationships
That are so vital, so important, so essential,
And so necessary.

We need to make new covenants,
New contracts, new agreements, new leagues,
New treaties, new engagements,
And new promises of mutual love and respect
From our most serious understanding.
It is this form of relationship that
Make human war, human violence
And bloodshed less demanding.
It is this form of genuine relationships
That will make true love and peace
A necklace to wear around our necks.
For thousands of years we have all
Waited for this day.
Our long waiting within
This period of separation from
The righteousness of God
Has determined for us the degree of our love
In our relationship with darkness
Of evil and unrighteousness.
Now that waiting time is over
And our love for the pure
Righteousness of God is strong
And is far beyond reconsideration.
Therefore the differences are now sinking
Into insignificance and our relationship
With the righteousness of God's
Divine love is saved.
When our long weird experience of
A conjugal union in spiritual darkness
Without love has been for us like a body without
A soul and the sooner our relationship
With evil is ended the better

The world will be.

After thousands of years
Of humanity living with a bent mind
Running in a mad race for power
Wealth, pleasure, and material comforts,
A race full of those blinded by their greed
For the material things of this world
Spiritually lost for 60 long centuries
And those in power think they need penitentiaries
When the truth of which is needed
Is the eyes to see God's Divine Love
With a strong upright mind
At the head of the whole of humanity.

As time passes with us standing
On the brink of the future
I cast my thoughts among nations with fragments
Of my spirit in the streets of all their cities.
I calmly invite humanity to a peaceful
Meditation and a serious contemplation
Of our dreadful past
And as we see the formation
Of memories standing in the ranks
In our minds by the millions
Look at where we all went wrong O' humanity
This is no time to throw stones.

The time for evil is gone.
Let us use the power of our retrospection
To look inward for the mighty change of direction.
So that when we look from the inside out

We will be able to see
The unique success of our Mighty destiny
As we review the words of the prophets
Of the Holy Scriptures
Words which carry a wide significance
Applicable to all of our short comings
Though many of their predictions

Have been clothed in allegorical language
Yet the prophet's predictions
Cover all shades of our life today.
Though we face the crushing defeat of evil times
We must master the psychological strength
To deal with the heavy forces moving toward us
From the past 6 thousand years.

From Adam to Moses to Jesus to Muhammad
6 thousand years of murder
From Cain to our very presence
Of murder and lies.
Though we existed in gross transgressions
Against the will of God
The yearning of our love must not be
For the evil things in this world's life.
We must not let sin be the cause
Of the vanquishing of our good intentions.
Though our development was in darkness
We have indeed come in touch
With the light of the Holy Word of God.
We are undoubtedly in the time
When we have attained to
The age of discretion

And know that now it is time
For us to take our stand.

This mighty change was
Introduced to the world from time to time
And we all marvel in our expressions as to how.
The words of the Holy Prophets
Removed many deficiencies from our lives
To suit the needs of
The new times to come.
Though we all walked upon this earth
For thousands of years
We never rose above our earthly concerns
Our thoughts never rising higher
Than our own personal set
Of vain desires and circumstances.
Many will never see that
Our own blood children are our own future
That will bring on this earth
The coming generations of men and women.
As men we never looked into the distant future
Which is within the soul of our women.
We never truly saw that our children
Are the treasures from the earth of the
Womb of our women.

My friend, I cannot reject this extreme view
For I must reach for my
Highest stage of development
Which is obtaining and maintaining
The possession of the great
Qualification called steadfastness.

I am at the point beyond all doubt.
This is our time of a terrific explosion.
We can see that the whole world
Has experienced a long dark night
And we are being made to pass
Into the great day of God's Divine Light
And everlasting Love.
We have been at the bottom
Of this U.S. Social Structure
Where we enjoyed little or no
Political or social rights.
Disgraced and degraded,
Despised and disregarded,
Rejected and debased,
We had become obscure and unimportant,
Deprived of privileges and permissions,
Seeing our unity was always broken by separation.

We have never experiences the
Guarantee of good treatment.
Been denied the knowledge
Of our course in time
And the practice of our own
Customs and traditions
Forced to make sacrifices and
Contributions of lifetimes of energy,
Time, and labor, forced to live in the
Ditch of entranced and entrenched
Inhuman conditions.
We come through long hard, weary times,
Forced to dwell in a
Strange land among strangers.

A strange environment,
Strange linguistics and consistent
Modification of influences
Which produces in us hatred,
Envy, self-destruction and
Almost physical death on several occasions.

But even in our early development
Signs of social stratification
Was at the top or peak
Of our torment and oppression
Along with our nobility.
Certainly we can prove that we
Descended from the
Negro Slave of North America.
We do not have our
Behinds on our shoulders.
We are living descendants of the
Same ancestors and we know
That our Ancient Ancestors
We're not only kingdom builders of
Good clean civilizations

But they, in their marvelous beauty
Were actually the Origin of Nobility.

God Himself whose own heart
In the beginning
Was long before all creation.

It is absolutely amazing to see
How the whole world has become blind.

Lost by the greatest deception
In human history
"One race is greater than the other
Because of its color?
Psychologically, the whole world
Is now upside down.
Evil lies have become supreme
Above righteousness and truth.
I find it hard to believe
That my insight is wrong.
I do not believe that my knowledge is confused.
The view of this world
Concerning the condition of this
Present humanity is not superstitious rhetoric,
Or inaccurate, nor incomplete.
The view of this world
Becoming enhanced with beauty
And value simply because I am
Constantly decorating my mind with the jewels
Of Universal Truth and now I see
It's my time to take my stand
When the spirit of the dead
Is found in the libraries of the world
I am inclined to study unrelentingly,
Tenaciously, and entrenching my superhuman
Capacity to reconcile my own mind
To deal with contradictory evil character
And characteristics now prevailing
Intellectually from high degrees of controversies

And even higher expressions in
Other dimensions of

Satan's deepest deception.
Money has become the god of the whole world
And we're trapped in the syndrome
Of evil, lies, corruption, illusions, and delusions.
Blind to the truth of the True and Living God.
Growing up in this wild sinful wilderness
Of North America, thinking that GOD
Was a mystery and that money
Was the road to true freedom

Behold, time has passed
And from our long journeys inward
The spirit of our own ancestors
Is the source of our power to our
Earthly and worldly prerogative
As we deal with our earthly predecessors.
We have dominion over our lives,
Our mental grounds, and
Our spiritual waters.
We are the rulers of our own atmosphere.
And for the first time
We are now entering into
That great communication with
The souls of our great ancestors
And the only true and Living God
No longer a mystery.
The spirit of our ancestors has
Brought me to this climax
My cohesiveness with them has
Now elegantly woven proclivity in the
Fibers of my being.
I can feel the spirits of the Holy Men of God

Prophets, messengers, and warners
Even those who died in the
Freedom struggle in North America

During the immediate past 5 centuries
I hear the voice of black angels
Singing lullabies and sacred melodies
Which often embrace my heart
With highly developed rhythms.
This abundance of evidence
Is sufficient to support my view
That love is the most
Basic element of human life
And I know it is now time for
Us to take a stand.

THEY CRITICIZE AND CONDEMN

They criticize and condemn
You and me!
They criticize and condemn
You and me,
The living product and manifestation
Of BLACK HISTORY!

My birth certificate identifies me
As an American Negro
Born in the Deep South
Born in a slave shack surrounded
By cotton fields.
Born into a family
Trained to live in FEAR.
Born a member of the race who
Slaved in America 310 years
From 1555 until 1863.
The worst crimes ever on earth
Were committed against you and me.

In 1863 when they declared
The slaves to be free
They were jumping for joy of
National Happiness.
All the slaves felt that
They had been blessed.
Able to run around ignorant
To the knowledge of self
Here in the west.
The spiritual dark world

Where the slaves found no rest.
Another 150 years of misery,
Pain, and tears,
Hard times, hard trials, and test,

Lost in mental darkness.
Blind, deaf, and dumb to
BLACK HISTORY
Another 150 years of time
Making mockery.
They laugh, they criticize
And condemned you and me.
And for simple mistakes
They hung us on a tree,
Yet they continue to deny us
The knowledge of our history.

HERE WE ARE TODAY
Working in America
Living blind to our proper place
In time.
Walking, sitting, riding, and flying
Around in America and the world
IGNORANT and FULL OF FEAR
Shaking and trembling when
Black History Month gets here.
What a hell of a stunt
To permit the oldest people on Earth
To study their history for
Only one month.

It's sad, but it's true

America is spending billions
Today to keep us blind to the
Real knowledge of us in time
And history.
Yet they have the nerve to
CRITICIZE AND CONDEMN
YOU AND ME.

WHAT DO WE SEE?

Trouble on the rise for you and me
Beyond world troubles
A glorious destiny?
Six thousand years of wars in our history.
Beyond seven thousand years
In the past Black people ruled
In kingdoms of peace.

Behold!
The distant Black Kingdom
Of ancient times
Behold!
The distant Black Civilizations
Built by the wisest minds
Behold!
The destroyers of our kingdoms
Who destroyed our memories
And even the long line of signs.
Behold!
The modern educational programs
Designed to keep a whole black nation blind.

We see tears rolling down the cheeks
Of a mighty black nation.
We see hurt in the heart of
A mighty black people
Who once established the stars of heaven
For an ancient occupation.

We see sorrow gripping the hearts of black parents

Of ancient civilizations.
We see the black children of God
In the west rising from the great tribulation.

WHEN THE TIDES CHANGE

When the tides change
People will never be the same.
Men and women all over the world,
Little boy and little girls,
People all over the world
Are afraid of what they see.
Everybody is struggling to be free.

But when the tides change
People will never be the same.

Discrimination, degeneration is what
We're all able to see.
The spirit of evil won't let nobody be.
Confusion of the past generations
Has destroyed many families.
Hunger, starvation, and thousands of diseases,
The spirits of evil
Are doing many things
We just can't believe

But when the tides change
People will never be the same.

Nations of the earth
Are preparing for the final war.
Playing with guns and bombs
Like children playing with toys.
People are partying and dancing
When the world is about

To be destroyed.
Paying no attention
To the enemy
And what he enjoys.

But when the tides change
People will never be the same

The spirits of evil
Are playing in the sky
While people are looking for drugs
Trying to get high.

Bombing planes and satellites
Seems to be our friends
But God is telling us
This is the final end
And maybe you don't believe,
But this reality

But WHEN THE TIDES CHANGE
People will never be the same.

WHAT'S GOING ON IN THE CITIES

EARLY in the morning
When the sun begins to shine
Casting powerful light
Waking up every human mind.
Setting the cities in motion
By the thousands at a time.
Every mind is turned on
Even criminals for crime.

WHAT'S GOING ON IN THE CITIES?

Freeways are crammed
People in a hurry.
All kinds of traffic jams
Early in the morning.
In the middles of the day
Late in the evening
People getting off of work
Ready to go.
Everybody can see
The sun sinking low.

WHAT'S GOING ON IN THE CITIES?

Night begins to fall
Crime begins to crawl.
Behind closed doors and city walls
Thousands of attractions
Millions of transactions,
Conversations,
Communications,

115

Automation, and
Transportation
People beginning brand new relations.

WHAT'S GOING ON IN THE CITIES?

Planes in the sky
Flying beneath the stars above.
Millions of people
Going behind closed doors
Everybody making love
Sleeping all night long.
Sleeping all night long.
Resting for the brand
New day to begin
So you and your friends
Can repeat
The same thing
All over again!

WHAT'S GOING ON IN THE CITIES?

THE HIGH COST OF LIVING

Everybody is working
Hard every day.
Everybody desires
To be giving
But it's hard to survive
With the high cost of living.

Working in the day,
Going to school at night
Trying to make ends meet
With all your might.

Struggling for higher wages
By developing your skills.
No time for pleasure
Because you're struggling TO live.
Inflation keeps you dealing
With the high cost of living.

Prices on everything today
Are much higher
Than they ever were before.
Sometimes you feel like crying
As you leave the grocery store.
Mouths to feed
You don't get much for your dollar
High prices giving you the chills,
Sometimes you just want to holler.
Inflation keeps you dealing with
The high cost of living.

ANOTHER EPISODE, ANOTHER EXPERIENCE

It's so hard to explain
What happiness really is

It's so hard to understand
Each stage of life
That we live.

It's so hard to see love
Except by what we give.

It's so hard to know time
Except by events that are real.

It's just another episode,
Another experience,
Another thrill, and another year.

As time passes us by
What can we will?

Will we ever wish for the days
That are rolling over our heads?

Will a time ever come
That we all shall dread?

Will we miss seeing
The value of people
And things
In passing moments?

It's just another episode,
Another experience,
Another thrill and another year.

Shall we cherish the seasons
And all the things they bring?

Shall we cherish the melodies
Of all the birds
And people that sing?

Shall we employ reasoning
To simple things
In time that have meaning?

Shall we walk peaceful roads
Of tomorrow?

It's just another episode,
Another experience,
Another thrill and another year.

When will the day come
When our battle for love is won?

Everybody was born
To enjoy freedom!
Everybody was born
To enjoy success.

IF THIS MEANS HAPPINESS

THEN NOBODY WAS BORN TO BE
OPPRESSED.

But what do we know?

It's just another episode,
Another experience
Another thrill and another year.

MR. INCOME, COME ON IN

Hey, Mr. Income
You're my best friend.
My pockets are empty
Where have you been?

I want to fly
Through the air
And ride through the wind.
I been so broke
Till the world
Looked like it was
Coming to an end.

I've been sitting at home
Singing a song.
I know something is wrong
All my money is gone
Mr. Income,
You're my best friend
So don't stand outside, please

MR. INCOME,
COME RIGHT ON IN.

Sometimes it's hard for me to think
Because I know that
I don't have no money in the bank
With the high cost of living
It's hard to survive.
My credit is so bad

Until I can't even borrow a dime.
You're my best friend

Don't you stand outside,
Come right on in.
Mr. Income please understand
I'm a hard-working man.
I'll make a living
Anyway I can;
But it's hard to find a job.

I wake up every morning
Facing all kinds of odds.
I go down to the employment office,
I don't have enough change
To buy myself
A cup of coffee.

You're my best friend.
Don't you stand outside
MR. INCOME,
Please come on in.

THE FINAL POET

THE FINAL POET

WHEN!
The winds of time have swept for
Over trillions of years
The storm of my life has been stilled by
The cold kiss of death

But as I stand within these mighty walls of time
I say to the worlds
You don't know the honor it gives me
To reveal to you

From among the past trillions of years,
The Final Poet.

THE FINAL POET
Don't put on no show
He's too busy telling the world
What the world don't know.
When you listen to his words
And your mind starts cracking
It's only because the problems in the world
Are continuously stacking and stacking.

THE FINAL POET
Don't have time to mack
His lips are too busy speaking the facts.
Mack men don't have the eyes to see
The world or things that's lacking
Mack men only see things in the world.
Plenty of money and pretty women
And their lips start smacking.
While military men are all over the world
Traveling, trucking, and tracking
Mack men are shacking, smacking, macking,
And can't see what they are lacking.
The final poet
Is about proving that the rulers
Of this world don't have good sense
If the rulers would be kind enough to confess
That the rulers are the reason
The world is in a mess.

People were created to live in peace under the sun

But the rulers are spending billions and trillions
Of the people's money on guns and bombs.
Every 24 house the rulers are in a mad race for power

The Final Poet's words
Don't insult the rulers' intelligence
The words of the Final Poet
Are a hanging rope around the neck
Of the rulers arrogance.

Kings of the Earth! What are they worth! WHEN
They're ready to cast millions of human beings
Under mountains of dirt!
Rulers, Kings, Pharaohs, and Presidents today
Are the worst there ever was,
They're ready to drench thousands of
Towns and cities into rivers of blood.

The rulers of this world are without heart
They're ready to turn the earth into a giant graveyard.
While the sun is burning over a thousand miles per
Hour, the earth is turning
The ignorant masses think they are learning
But in reality, the masses are only yearning.

The masses of this world are blind
And cannot see through the dark clouds of lies
False promises and tricks in the treaties of peace.

The masses are sitting at home
Listening to the radio and television
Believing in the wicked rulers and their decisions.

You shouldn't tell me that I'm going to blow it.
It's my job, baby, because
I'm the Final Poet.

Don't tell me that I'm reading this
From some kind of a book
When all you need to do is take a second look.
The world you live in is about to be shook
It's the last supper for the world
And God is the cook.

You might say I'm losing my mind
But the visions of The Final Poet say
The worlds has fallen
Into the most evil of times

I don't wish to disturb your dreams
But the vast, drastic, dreadful, destruction
Is at a magnitude the world has never seen.
RACISM... CAPITALISM...CMMUNISM
Are about and bound to collide
Like ships riding the waves of the oceans
Over a mile in the sky
All because the rulers are wicked
Controlling the earth with their
GREED... VANITY... ARROGANCE... AND PRIDE
The Final Poet
Don't have time for telling lies
He's too busy exposing the secret thoughts,
Evil plans, and wicked intention that
Lies in the ruler's minds.

The ruler's imaginations are in flames
And you can tell that the mind of the rulers
Are swimming around in psychological
RED WAVES OF HELL
While second and third class criminals are trapped
In state and federal prisons, insane asylums,

And county jails, the burning of human flesh
The world will soon be forced to smell.

The masses got a pain in the brain
Immorality is driving millions insane.
The rulers are claiming that the world is in for
A better and brighter change
While introducing the masses to a brand new game.
The earth is traveling around the sun
Like a train on a track
Immorality is reality and that is fact.

They say 20 centuries ago
A holy Man was killed by crucifixion
And died upon a cross.
20 centuries later evil rulers are the boss.
Everybody believing in them seems to be lost.
We should let the Holy Man rest in peace
The knowledge of his mind
We all can see.
The rulers had doubt and tried to put the light out
Now, the masses are crying out for help
From a Holy Man
The rulers put to death.

Let your light shine from your human mind
And encounter and attack
From the rulers of mankind
The rulers want darkness
For the sake of keeping the masses blind.
So their evil works won't stop
As long as the earth is traveling around the sun
Spinning like a top
The masses are groping in darkness
Because the masses' minds are shot.
The rulers are playing tricks while
The masses are taking a fix.
Immorality is reality, the whole world is sick.

The Final Poet
Brings the rulers under
The masses' magnifying glass
So the masses can see who it is
That keeps the masses living in the past
The rulers keep the masses on earth paying high rent
When the Creator of land and water
Don't charge the rulers one red cent.
The masses on the earth
Are going to the ruler's churches and schools
Solely and slowly becoming
The ruler's tools and fools
Merely for the rulers to use and to rule.

The rulers aren't thrilled
When the real truth is revealed.
The leading men and women of truth

The rulers would just love to kill.
But men and women of truth
Are not afraid of death they depend on
The Creator of heaven and earth for help.
The men and women of truth
Desire the will of the Creator

Which is humanity's moral reconstruction
But every government on earth is full of corruption
THE WHOLE WORLD HAS ROLLED INTO
THE JAWS OF DESTRUCTION.
THE FINAL POET
Is just an aid who is not afraid of giving
The men and women of the truth his help.
He is working hard to do all he can
Before he meets the heavenly Angel of death.
Destruction is coming soon
And as it was written
NOTHING OF THIS EVIL WORLD WILL BE LEFT.

So before I'm dead, I'll never dread
One word of the things I've said.
I'm trying to be nice
By not having to say these things twice.
The rulers have hearts colder than ice
The rulers control the masses
In a psychological vice.

The masses don't believe in using aggression
So the rulers keep controlling the masses
With evil lies, tricks, false promises,
And oppression,

Of course, at the Ruler's discretion.
You shouldn't be surprised
Go on and open your eyes
Because everything you see was
Foretold and prophesied.
Take a real good look in the world,
It's like reading a book

Can't you read between the lines?
Can't you see the signs of the time?
Otherwise never mind, your ignorance will do just fine
But remember it's your fault
For pretending like you're blind.

God hates sin.
Sin is God's biggest enemy
So the world is about to die,
God has started cry.
His number one Angel called death is now
Ready to kiss the whole world good bye.
People are unable to see
How God really feels about immorality.

Death comes soon with the final consequence
At a time when the nations shall be downing and
Drenched in blood the nations will
Look like the Red Sea
It's only the world's future reality
Produced by the world's immorality.

You must open your eyes and see the factuality.
God is so angry with evil and immorality.

Freak games, orgies, and sex changes and
Adultery, fornication, motel and hotel legislation,
Houses of legalized prostitution!
Motels are for the adulterous fornicating poor
Hotels are for middle class, the rich and wealthy.
Immorality's making everybody unhealthy.

It's the diseased flood of burning anger
In the eyes of the people you meet.
Disease and anger flowing in the streets
Wives and husbands are guilty and weak.
Women becoming rough and tough

Men becoming tender and sweet
Immorality is a vice and a fix
The masses are swimming in corruption
THE WHOLE WORLD IS SICK.

NOW DEATH IS TRAVELLING
All over the world snatching souls
From the brave and the bold
Leaving dead bodies all over the globe
Stretched out cold
I think about the exciting stories death has told
Every 24 hours thousand are losing their breath
Crying to the rulers, trying to help.

North Pole, South Pole
Death is still snatching souls.
Moving Far East and deep into the west
With a report of ones losing their breath.

Every time death comes in out the wind
To visit his Final Poetic friend
One blink of the eye, death is gone again.
Moving in cities, villages and towns
All over the land.
One blink of the eye, death is surrounded
By bare, rugged hills
And trackless miles of desert sand
Knocking thousands of planes out of the skies
Millions of people dropping like flies.

Guns and bombs are no match
For rain, hail or snow storms.
Helicopters, airplanes, and jets
will lose radio communications.
Airplane disasters death is moving faster

Missiles and rockets
Totally destroyed in hurricane pockets.
Airplanes and jets coming in contact
With the largest tornadoes they ever met.
Tons of ocean water
Being dumped on fleets of ships
All Death does is put his hands on his hips
While listening to the sound
Down on the ground.
Rulers and the Masses are being removed
From all their worries
Volcanoes and earthquakes
Turning thousands of towns and cities
Into giant cemeteries

IS THIS THE END!
GOD SAID
SAVE THE BABES
LET'S START ALL OVER AGAIN!!!

Don't get angry with me
For trying to show it.
It's my job, baby!

I'm
THE FINAL POET

Thoughts of Augustus

Made in the USA
Columbia, SC
27 June 2021